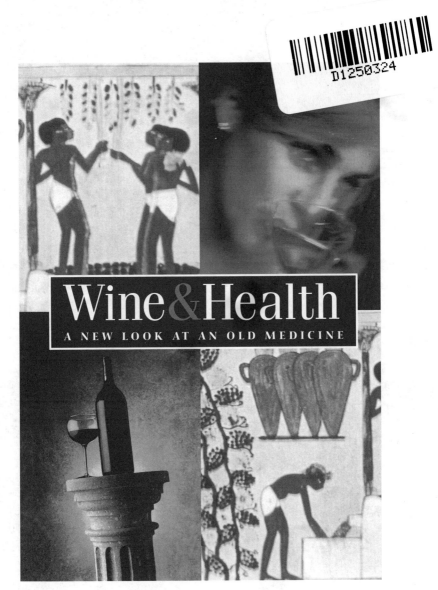

# Wine&Health
## A NEW LOOK AT AN OLD MEDICINE

# DR PHILIP NORRIE

# Wine&Health

## A NEW LOOK AT AN OLD MEDICINE

APOLLO BOOKS

This book is dedicated to
my wife Belinda and
sons Andrew and Alexander.

*Published by*
C. Pierson, Publishers
PO Box 87
Mosman NSW 2088
Australia

First published 2000
Text Copyright © Dr Philip Norrie

ISBN O 947068 35 X

ILLUSTRATIONS *Cover, title page, pages 18 and
20-21;* courtesy of Professor N. Kanawati,
The Australian Centre for Egyptology, with
thanks to Beth Thompson. *Page 25;* photo by
Carol Gibbons. *Page 28;* courtesy of The
Royal Australasian College of Physicians,
History of Medicine Library. *Title page;*
Part of the ceiling of the Chapel of the
Noble Sennefer depicting grape vines and
the tomb owner and his wife.

*Design* Di Quick
*Print* Pirie Printers, Canberra

# CONTENTS

# ABOUT
# THE AUTHOR

Dr Philip Norrie was born in Sydney, Australia in 1953. He attended Knox Grammar School and graduated from the University of New South Wales Medical School in 1977. He is a General Practitioner at Elanora and lives at Palm Beach on Sydney's northern beaches with his wife Belinda and two sons.

Dr Norrie has a keen interest in medical history, especially as it relates to man's oldest medicine, wine. His writing includes *Australia's Wine Doctors*, an account of Australian doctors who have established vineyards, the histories *Dr Lindeman* (1993), *The Penfold Wine Group* (1994) and *Leo Buring* (1996), an account of the early wine industry in and around Sydney, *Vineyards of Sydney* (1990) and *Dr Philip Norrie's Advice on Wine and Health—Thinking & Drinking Health. Dr Philip Norrie's Wine and Health Diary* is published annually.

Dr Norrie graduated Master of Science from The University of Sydney in 1993. His thesis was the history of the McLeay family involvement in the early wine industry of New South Wales.

In 1998, he completed a Master of Social Science (Hons) at Charles Sturt University, Wagga Wagga. His thesis was the contribution made to Australian wine making by Leo Buring.

His research into the history of wine as a medicine is the subject of his Doctorate of Philosophy at the University of Western Sydney, where he lectures on wine and health.

Philip Norrie is the Australian representative on the Editorial Board of *Alcohol in Moderation* (AIM), an independent journal which reviews scientific literature on alcohol and health and is a member of the Vinopolis Wine Advisory Board. He has written the wine and health segments in the *Oxford Companion to Wine* and writes regualr wine and health articles for the *Wine Hunter, Winestate, New Asia Cuisine and Wine Scene* magazines.

Dr Norrie has developed a 20-hectare vineyard, Pendarves Estate, on his property at Belford in the Lower Hunter Valley of New South Wales. Set on the unique Belford dome of limestone, Pendarves Estate produces award-winning Chardonnay, Verdelho, Sauvignon Blanc, Pinot Noir, Shiraz, Chambourcin and Merlot-Malbec-Cabernet wines.

# FOREWORD

## BY ROBERT MONDAVI
## NAPA VALLEY, CALIFORNIA

I began taking an interest in wine and its health benefits around 1950. It was then that the first rigorous medical research began to demonstate that moderate consumption of wine had positive health outcomes.

In the United States there were groups totally opposed to the consumption of wine and any form of alcohol, that did not believe these findings. These groups would not accept even the most rigorous and detailed scientific research.

Since 1950, through the continuing work of many scientists, reseachers and industry spokes-people, including the work of Dr Philip Norrie, the scientific findings that there are health benefits from moderate wine consumption, has changed the views of many former sceptics and non-believers.

I know that for all those interested in wine, involved in the wine trade, or for those consumers who simply enjoy a glass of wine, *Wine and Health: A New Look at an Old Medicine* will be an excellent guide and an enjoyable education.

# FOREWORD

## BY ROBERT LUSBY
## PROFESSOR OF VASCULAR SURGERY,
## UNIVERSITY OF SYDNEY

The consumption of wine has been connected with good health since ancient times, particularly in Mediterranean countries. The grape vine through the ages has been symbolically linked to rebirth, since it flourishes in spring. Indeed, the consumption of wine has often brought people into communion with each other and also with their gods.

The celebrated Greek physician, Hippocrates (450–370 BC) prescribed wine as a wound dressing, as a purgative, as a diuretic, as a nourishing dietary beverage and as a cooling agent for fevers. These practices continued through to the Middle Ages. The decline in wine consumption after the Middle Ages in England can be attributed to the Puritan religious movement led by Oliver Cromwell, who destroyed the vineyards of England after he came to power between 1650 and 1658. The Puritan movement spread to the New World (USA) when the Pilgrim Fathers settled the east coast of North America in 1620. This Puritan movement in England and the USA eventually led to the Temperance movement of the 19th century, which condemned alcohol in all forms and culminated in the Prohibition movement in the USA in the 1920s.

Today we turn to the French paradox: a surprising lack of cardiovascular disease in a large number of the French population who eat a fat-saturated diet, have little exercise and continue to smoke, but for whom red wine is an integral part of their diet. The moderate consumption of red wine appears to afford them protection. This observation of the apparent good health of the people of Southern Europe was also made by James Busby, the prophet of the Australian wine industry. In 1830 he recommended to the colonists of New South Wales that they assimilate the habits of the Southern Europeans in respect of wine, which he referred to as *'the more natural, more wholesome drink prepared from the pure juice of the grape'*, rather than *'consume the strong brandied preparations which contributed to the ill-health of the Northern Europeans'*.

We are currently looking for the scientific evidence as to why wine — in particular red wine — should be so beneficial. Antioxidants such as polyphenols, resveratrol and quercetin are readily identified in red wines. These substances have the potential to alter the blood lipids in a favourable way and prevent the development of atheromatous plaque which can obstruct our arteries. Flavonoids contained in the red grape skins are preserved in the alcohol and then released to also produce a positive effect when ingested. Research such as the *Copenhagen Study,* which demonstrates a 50 per cent reduction in cardiovascular death amongst moderate wine drinkers, highlights the importance of moderate wine consumption to the health of the general population.

*Wine and Health: A New Look at an Old Medicine* looks through the ages at the benefits of wine consumption to physical and psychological health. It establishes the necessity to consider once again the use of wine as a medicine and as an aid to wellbeing.

# INTRODUCTION

## WINE: THE THINKING PERSON'S HEALTH DRINK

The purpose of this book is to help you to die young as late as possible; in other words to recommend how it is possible to have a healthy, youthful body for as long as possible and increase both quality and quantity of life.

Its purpose is to also alter the perception that wine is only a drink for special occasions but can and should be consumed daily, as a health drink, to add 'enjoyment' to a healthy, disease free life.

*Wine & Health: A New Look at an Old Medicine* presents the facts about the use of wine as a medicine by the medical profession in the past and the results of current research into the benefits of moderate wine consumption on people's health today.

## AN INGREDIENT IN A HEALTHY LIFESTYLE

Wine is man's oldest medicine, having been used as such by the medical profession for more than 5000 years. Wine is also our most documented medicine, its virtues recorded by the original wine scribes, who were doctors prescribing its use thousands of years ago.

Consumed in moderation, wine is our most potent preventative medicine; it has the potential to reduce death rates from all causes by up to 50 per cent. There is no man-made, patented medicine that can claim as high a success rate as can the consumption of wine in moderation. Consuming wine in moderation is, in fact, the most important preventative health measure one can take, with the exception of ceasing to smoke, as it reduces our death rate from vascular disease by up to 50 per cent and cancer by up to 24 per cent. It also reduces stress levels by acting as a relaxant.

Vascular and stress-related diseases are the two greatest causes of illness in Western society. The biggest killer is vascular disease, in the form of heart attacks and strokes, which account for up to half the death rate. Vascular disease can be largely prevented by lifestyle changes including not smoking, reducing excess weight, lowering blood pressure, treating diabetes, exercising, eating less fat, lowering cholesterol, eating high fibre foods such as fruit and vegetables and lowering stress levels. It is simply unrealistic, however, to expect that most people will comply with these important lifestyle demands for the rest of their life. It is more realistic to encourage people to regularly enjoy some wine with dinner. Medical research into the benefits of wine in the past decade has shown that consuming wine in moderation is the best way to prevent vascular disease. It is also an easier demand to make in the modification of people's lifestyles.

Over the past four decades doctors have treated vascular disease with various new forms of surgery from bypasses to angioplasty — inserting balloons to push open the blockages in the disease-causing blood vessels. Today the emphasis of medicine is turning towards the prevention of vascular disease. Wine has the potential to play a vital role in this.

## LEADING A LONGER, DISEASE-FREE LIFE

Consuming wine in moderation should be incorporated into any preventative approach to healthcare. Abstaining from wine may in fact be a factor in increasing the risk of vascular disease.

Research currently underway across the world is taking a new look at our oldest medicine in its various forms. Wine has been used in the past as an antiseptic, reducing the rate of infection, which in centuries past was the most common cause of death. Now wine is part of a medical revolution to prevent vascular disease and degenerative diseases such as cancer, which are the most common causes of death today.

Wine contains potent antioxidant properties which alter the fats and counter other harmful substances, or waste products known as free radicals, that cause these diseases. Consuming wine in moderation can potentially add years to life expectancy.

Both red and white wine convey benefits to our health. While red wines usually contain more antioxidants than white wines, both provide adequate antioxidant activity, the extra in red wine being redundant once 100 per cent antioxidant activity is reached. Recent studies by Dr Gordon Troup at Monash University, Dr Klaus Jung at Mainz University, Drs Vinson and Hontz of Scranton University and by the Jordan Heart Research Foundation in the United States have shown that white wine is just as effective as red wine as an antioxidant.

Wine is usually consumed as an accompaniment to food, where the most important point is that the correct wine variety is married to that food, not whether the wine is red or white. Wine consumed with food adds to the nutritional benefit of the food, while the absorption of the alcohol in the wine is slowed down by digestion of the food. This adds to the enjoyment and health benefits of wine. Both red and white wine are sources of sugars, proteins, antioxidants, vitamins and minerals.

## WHY ALL THE INTEREST IN WINE AND HEALTH?

The notion that consuming any form of alcohol is bad for you — the line taken by the influential anti-alcohol lobby, has now been proven false. Recent medical and scientific studies have shown that alcohol consumed in moderation is not only not detrimental to health, but that the moderate consumption of wine, in particular, has significant health benefits.

It's time to let everyone in on the secret. The good news of the health benefits of wine, as reported in numerous research articles, has been largely ignored by medical and scientific literature in the supposed interest of public health. It has been thought that to report the medical benefits of drinking wine may encourage alcohol abuse, a legitimate concern, but is it justified?

Research papers are being published regularly showing new medical benefits of consuming wine in moderation. In *Wine & Health: A New Look at an Old Medicine* this latest information is explained, letting everyone know the potential role of wine in the general maintenance of health.

## THE STORY OF WINE

Wine is a cerebral commodity for a host of reasons. For instance there is great interest in the different varieties, the vineyard terroir, that is, the aspect, location, soil and microclimate, the vintages and varying wine making techniques. Wine appreciation requires significant consideration to appreciate it fully. Wine in moderation could be considered the thinking person's health drink, giving increased quality and quantity of life.

The great 18th century French philosopher, Voltaire wrote about moderation; *'Use, do not abuse. Neither abstinence nor excess ever rendered man happy'*. He may well have been talking about wine.

The modern era of wine and health is illustrated in Australia in the 18th century. In 1787 the First Fleet sailed from England for Australia, using wine as a medicine and a source of vitamins to help convicts survive the long sea voyage. This tradition of Australian doctors' medical use of wine was the springboard for today's research into the relationship between wine and health.

The story of wine as a medicine begins in ancient times, moves through the centuries and the continents to Australia's wine doctors, and continues today with research into the role of wine in preventative medicine.

# ROYAL MEDICINE: WINE USED AS A MEDICINE THROUGH THE AGES

## AN HISTORICAL OVERVIEW OF THE MEDICINAL USES OF WINE

Viticulture, or grape growing probably began some 9 000 years ago in the region of Georgia, which lies on the eastern shores of the Black Sea, near the Caucasus Mountains. From here viticulture appears to have spread to the evolving cultures of the Middle East, with each adopting its own myth of the origins of wine. The grape vine travelled down the Tigris and Euphrates Rivers to Babylon and overland to Persia. It spread to Egypt and to Greece and was adopted by the ancient Greek and Roman empires, which spread viticulture throughout the Mediterranean. Viticulture continued to expand until most climatically favourable areas of Europe grew grapes.

Since the age of the Egyptian Pharaohs 5 000 years ago, wine has been used as a medicine. The ancient Egyptian, Greek and Roman empires all appreciated and utilised wine as medicine. Into the Middle Ages monks ran hospitals in their monasteries and made medicines from wine. These were the basis of many of the liqueurs enjoyed today.

## THE MIDDLE EAST

Wine is supposed to have been discovered in Persia (now Iran) by the mistress of King Jamshid, who was so fond of grapes that he had them stored in jars so that he could eat them all year round. One year, the grapes fermented in a jar and were no longer sweet; he assumed the new liquid in the bottom of the jar was poisonous and marked the jar accordingly. His mistress, so the story goes, had such a bad headache that she wanted to die, so she drank the liquid in the 'poisonous' jar. The wine made her feel better, greatly easing her pain and enabling her to fall asleep. Upon hearing of this miraculous cure King Jamshid tested the 'poison' himself and enjoyed the wine so much that the wonderful tonic was named the Royal Medicine. Wine was then held in the highest esteem by the Persians for its curing qualities.

*Part of a wall scene from the tomb of Nikauisesi at Saqqara, Egypt.*
*It depicts offering bearers dragging jars containing four different types of wine.*

This accidentally concocted wine was a result of the simple process of fermentation. All that is required to make basic wine is to crush grapes into a vessel and allow the natural yeast present on the grape skins to ferment the crushed grape juice. Eventually wine will be produced, which can be drained from the skins, and consumed.

Armenian wine sellers spread the knowledge of wine making down the River Euphrates to Babylon (now Iraq), where the Sumerian culture began around 4000 BC. The oldest known medical handbook, a Sumerian pharmacopaeia written on a clay tablet dated approximately 2200 BC, recommends the use of wine as treatment for ailments, making wine man's oldest documented medicine. Sweet wine mixed with honey, for instance, was used to treat coughing. Tabatu was a Babylonian medical drink made from water and small amounts of fermented fruit juice or wine.

*Hippocrates (460–377 BC) was the leading Greek physician of the ancient world and author of the Hippocratic oath.*

There are many examples from ancient times, for instance Ptah-
Hotep, the vizier of ancient Egypt, was highly regarded for his
wisdom and literary achievements, lived at Memphis in North Egypt
about 4000 BC. In his tomb are the oldest known inscriptions
depicting wine making. Egyptian papyri dating from 2000 BC also
record the medicinal use of wine. Wine made from grapes, dates
and palm sap was used as a solvent for mixing other medicines

*A scene in the Chapel of Sennefer, Thebes, during the New Kingdom. It depicts the grape harvest and pressing of wine.*

including, for example, treatment for an infected ear, where wine was used as an antiseptic.

Islamic doctors, restricted by the teachings of the Koran, used wine for medicinal purposes only. Leading Arabian doctors through the first millennium including Rhazes (860–932 AD), Avicenna (980–1032 AD) known as the "Prince of Physicians", and Albucasis (936–1013 AD) used wine to prevent infection in wounds.

## THE MEDITERRANEAN

In the Middle East, wine as a medicinal remedy had been prescribed in a form diluted three to five times by water. The ancient Greek physicians were the first to prescribe wine undiluted; it was one of their most used medicines. Hippocrates (460–377 BC), a leading physician in the ancient world, is recognised as the father of modern Western medicine. He was the first to claim that illness was not due to the wrath of the gods but due to poor nutrition or disease. He wrote of using wine extensively, *'as a wound dressing, as a nourishing dietary beverage, as a cooling agent for fevers, as a purgative and as a diuretic'*. He made distinctions between the various types of wine, described their different effects, directed their uses for specific conditions, advised when they should be diluted with water and, in addition, stated when wine should be avoided. In an essay on wounds, Hippocrates wrote: *'no wound should be moistened with anything except wine, unless the wound is in a joint'*.

*Galen (131–210 AD), was a prominent Greek physician of his time and an advocate for the use of wine to cleanse wounds.*

Regarding the therapeutic uses of wine, Hippocrates noted that the yeast and unaltered sugar of new wines were irritants of the gastrointestinal tract; white, thin and acid wines were the more diuretic and wines rich in tannin were anti-diarrhoeic. Hippocrates said of wine as medicine: *'Wine is fit for man in a wonderful way provided that it is taken with good sense by the sick as well as the healthy'*.

Even after the ascent of Rome in 200 BC Greek physicians still dominated the world of medicine, but they were not trusted by the Romans, who thought they were possible poisoners or assassins. Asclepiades of Bithyria (124–40 BC), a Greek physician who established Greek medicine in Rome, recommended fresh air, light, appropriate diet, hydrotherapy, massage and exercise. A pioneer in the humane treatment of mental disorders, he used occupational therapy, music, exercises and wine to calm his patients. Appointed physician to the Roman statesman Cicero (106–43 BC), he wrote an essay describing the virtues of Greek and Roman wines, entitled *'Concerning the Dosage of Wine'*.

Aurelius Cornelius Celsus (25 BC–37 AD), a leader of Roman medicine and author of the medical tome *De Medicina*, wrote about the therapeutic uses of wines from different regions of Italy, Sicily and Greece. He wrote: *'Those who have a slow digestion and for that reason get a distended abdomen, or because of some kind of fever feel thirst during the night, they should, before going to bed, drink three or four cups of wine through a thin straw.'*

Dioscorides was a Greek army surgeon under Roman emperor Nero (37–68 AD). He wrote *De Universa Medicina* in approximately 78 AD. While accompanying Roman armies on their expeditions he gathered information for his writings, describing various substances including wine, detailing their dietetic and therapeutic values. *'In general wine warms the body, it is digestible, increases the appetite, helps the sleep and has reviving properties'*, he wrote. Dioscorides became the founder of the study of medical substances as an applied science, called Materia Medica. He prescribed wine for many conditions, always specifying a particular type.

The well known Greek physician, Galen (131–201 AD) was a physician to the gladiators. He had to treat lacerations, stabbing wounds, amputations and evisceration — where the abdominal

*Rhazes (860–932 AD), an Arabian physician who was also a great advocate for the use of wine as a medicine.*

cavity has been punctured and the abdominal contents of bowel and organs are exposed. Galen, like Hippocrates, favoured the use of wine to prevent infection. He wrote of curing *'the most seriously wounded by covering the wounds by a wet cloth wet with astringent wine kept moist both day and night by a superimposed sponge'*. He would go to the extreme of soaking the exposed abdominal contents in wine before replacing them in the abdominal cavity in evisceration cases. *Galenicals* were drugs he devised from vegetables, most mixed with wine. Galen, whose thoughts dominated European medicine until the Middle Ages, wrote a catalogue of wines from different areas noting their chemical characteristics and physiological effects and advocated using wine as a suitable treatment for the diseases of the aged.

# MEDIEVAL MEDICINE

Monks were the primary healers in Medieval times. Their medicine was based on the classic Greek and Roman discoveries, with some Islamic influence. They chiefly used herbs and secondarily animal products. Wine was used as a medicine by itself or mixed with other compounds to make a palatable concoction from foul tasting substances. Monks preserved medical knowledge from the past in their libraries and advanced science and viticulture within the protection of their monasteries. Many of today's liqueurs owe their origin to medicines used by the monks in Medieval times: monasteries have developed their own famous liqueurs, such as D.O.M Benedictine, created in France in 1510.

Wine making techniques in Medieval times were poor. Wine suffered from oxidation because the art of sterile wine making was lost and air tight container production abandoned after Roman times. This resulted in secondary fermentation and oxidation in wine barrels and goat skins, turning the wine into vinegar. Wine in medieval times had to be drunk young, not aged, as the techniques of wine production did not allow ageing in cellars.

*D.O.M Benedictine Liqueur, originally produced in a
Benedictine Abbey. It was used by the monks for
250 years as a medicine for the sick and poor.*

*The interior ruins of the Colosseum, Rome. In Galen's time gladiators who fought here had their wounds bound with bandages soaked in wine.*

Outside the monasteries, Arnauld de Villeneuve (1235–1311), author of *Liber de Vinis*, was an advocate for the use of wine as a tonic, as part of a poultice — a moist application to the skin to improve circulation and treat inflamed areas — and as an antiseptic for sterilizing polluted water. He established the use of wine as a recognised therapy during the late Middle Ages.

Theodoric (1205–1296) also insisted that wine was the best possible dressing for wounds. He was the first to challenge the doctrine of 'laudable pus', which was the teaching and belief that the best method of treating a wound was to promote suppuration, the formation of pus and that the wound should be kept open. All this achieved was increased infection and subsequent death. Theodoric would wash the wound with wine, scrupulously removing every foreign particle and then bringing the edges of the wound together thus preventing infection and subsequent death.

Hieronymus Brunschwig (1450–1533) was a surgeon in the Alsation army who made his specialities the treatment of gunshot wounds and the distillation of alcohol. He promoted a mixture of strong Gascony wine, brandy and herbs called *'aqua vite composite'* for cleansing wounds, which was also used to *'cure palsy, putteth away ring-*

*worms, expel poison and it was most wholesome for the stomach, heart and liver. It nourisheth blood'.* He introduced distillation of spirits into England in 1525. The distilled spirit was originally used as a medicine, but when gin was widely distilled from sawdust and woodshavings it became a source for alcoholism and poisoning. Wine did not have this effect as it was made from pure healthy grapes.

The word alcohol was first used by the sixteenth century German medical teacher, Theophrastus Bombastus Von Hohenheim known as Paracelsus (1493–1541). The physicians of ancient Egypt had used the brittle metallic element, antimony, as a medicine. The Arabs called powdered antimony al-kohl. This word was then used to mean a fine substance and later the essence of a substance. Paracelsus applied this Arabian term to the spirit in wine, calling it alcohol because of its healing qualities. He popularised chemical medicine, the use of minerals as therapeutic agents, against the accepted followers of Galen who used plant medicines, hence he earned the title of 'father of pharmacology'. He is famous for stating that, *'whether wine is a nourishment, medicine or poison is a matter of dosage.'*

## POST MIDDLE AGES

After the Middle Ages wine was constantly prescribed for medicinal purposes. The leading English physician William Heberden (1710–1801) advocated the use of wine as an individual substance of benefit to health. As a result, the use of wine as a medicine increased in popularity among English doctors. In 1818 *Thomson's London Dispensatory* contained a chapter on wines, listing ten formulas for medicinal wine. *The British Pharmacopoeia,* as recently as a century ago, contained formulas using wine, sherry and brandy. Hospitals regularly used wine as a medicine. For example, the single biggest expenditure of Leicester Hospital, England, in 1773 was for wine for the patients. It follows that the English surgeon on board the First Fleet to Australia in 1787, John White, insisted on the availability of wine to assist in the maintenance of health of all those on board during the voyage.

Alcoholic drinks were also a safe alternative to polluted and cholera-infected water, and milk which often carried TB. The only

*Louis Pasteur (1822–1895) invented 'Pasteurization'.*
*He also did significant research into the fermentation process*
*of wine and beer that was of great economic value to France.*

safe, infection-free drink was alcoholic and the most therapeutic of the alcoholic drinks was wine, not spirits. Wine was described by the famous French microbiologist Louis Pasteur as *'the most health-ful of all beverages'*. Even as late as 1892 Professor Alois Pick of the Vienna Institute of Hygeine recommended adding wine to water to sterilize the water in the cholera epidemic of Hamburg. Research today shows that the reason wine is so much more effective as an antiseptic than pure alcohol is because wine contains other steril-izing compounds in addition to alcohol; polyphenols such as malvoside — the principal pigment in red wine — have a major anti-bacterial effect.

'*Astringent wines for diarrhoea, the white wines as diruretics, port in acute fevers and for anaemia, claret and burgundy for anorexia, cham-pagne for nausea and catarrhal conditions and port, sherry and madeira in convalescence*', wrote medical historian Dr Peter Burke in 1984 of how wine was prescribed as a medicine in the post Middle Ages.

# THE AUSTRALIAN
# EXPERIENCE

Many of Australia's premier wine producing companies were established by medical doctors, a trend begun by Dr William Redfern at Campbellfields, New South Wales and Sir John Jamison at Regentville in Sydney's outskirts in 1818. Australia's three largest wine companies were founded by doctors: Dr Henry John Lindeman founded Lindemans at Cawarra in 1843; Dr Christopher Rawson Penfold founded Penfolds at Magill in 1844; and Dr Alexander Kelly founded Tintara, the forerunner of Hardys in 1861. Other famous wine companies followed, including Angoves, Houghton, Stanley and Minchinbury, all established by doctors. So involved in viticulture have Australia's wine doctors been, that about two thirds of any vintage in Australia is crushed by wine companies founded by doctors.

The Australian experience started in 1787 when the First Fleet was preparing to sail from England for New South Wales. Surgeon John White, in charge of the health of all convicts, sailors, soldiers and free settlers, was not satisfied with the standard rations issued to the fleet. White wrote to Governor Phillip asking for what he called 'necessaries': items of food not included in the standard ration, including wine.

*The First Fleet arriving in Australia, January 1788.*

*Governor Philip raises the flag in Sydney Cove, 1788.*

White used wine as a medicine throughout the voyage to Australia to help to prevent malnutrition and disease. He wrote in his diary: *'On those days the scurvy began to show itself in Charlotte (one of the convict transport ships), mostly among those who had the dysentery to a violent degree; but I was pretty well able to keep it under by a liberal use of the essence of malt and some good wine, which ought not to be classed among the most indifferent antiscorbutics'.*

Medical treatment of convicts during transportation to Australia in the late 1700s and early 1800s was haphazard. Not all ships carried a doctor on board. Tragedy struck in 1814 when the Surrey left England carrying 200 male convicts, marine guards and crew.

Left *Dr William Redfern (1774–1833), ex-convict, became the personal physician to Governor Macquarie.* Right *Dr Alexander Kelly, wine author and founder of Hardy's 'Tintara' vineyard.*

*The cramped conditions of prisoners aboard a transport ship,*
*conditions that were ripe for the rapid spread of disease.*

The captain feared the convicts would take over the ship during the voyage so he had them closely confined in cells with poor ventilation and hygiene. Typhus, or gaol fever, took hold among the convicts, guards and crew, killing 51, a quarter of the ships company.

Governor Macquarie ordered an investigation into the conditions aboard the ship after arrival, appointing Dr William Redfern to the job. Redfern was Sydney's leading doctor and became Australia's first wine doctor when he established his vineyard, Campbellfields, to Sydney's south west in 1818. Redfern had also been a convict, transported to Australia on board Minerva in 1801 for his part in a mutiny aboard HMS Standard in 1797, while in the role of ship's surgeon.

The investigation, along with Redfern's findings and recommendations, was to have a marked impact on Australia's wine industry. Redfern had discovered the captain had withheld rations from the convicts, including their wine ration, so he could sell them at various ports on the way to Australia. Redfern found that basic necessities such as adequate clothing, food, water, wine and hygiene meant the difference between life and death for those aboard these ships.

In a letter to Governor Macquarie dated 30th September 1814, Redfern made eleven recommendations, to prevent further tragic voyages. They included that a quarter of a pint of wine with added lime juice be given to each convict each day, out in the open so no one could withhold their ration, to prevent malnutrition and scurvy. He also recommended that every transport ship have a properly qualified doctor on board.

Redfern's recommendations were acted upon immediately, and later published as 'Instructions for Surgeons, Superintendent on Board Convict Ships Bound for New South Wales or Van Diemens

Left *A young Dr Christpher Rawson Penfold (1811–1870), circa the 1830s was the founder of Penfolds wines in 1844.* Right *Governor Lachlan Macquarie.*

*Views of the 'Surrey', a typical ship used for the transportation of convicts from England to Australia, circa 1800.*

Land and for the Masters of Those Ships'. This book was standard issue to all transports, their masters and surgeons and was one of Australia's first public health documents.

## AUSTRALIA'S
## FIRST WINE DOCTORS

Australia became host to many naval surgeons, as they retired here to take advantage of better working prospects. Having worked on board convict transport and later, migrant transport ships, these doctors knew the benefits of wine which would, as Redfern put it, *'maintain the vigour of the system'* and *'dispel despondency'* among those confined below decks in prison cells. The quality of the wine available to them however, was relatively poor, because the better wines from Europe were kept by the English wine merchants and only the inferior wines were shipped out to Australia. By the time the wine had been six months in a leaking oak cask, in the bilge of a ship it would have been at great risk of oxidation and sea-water contamination. To secure a good supply of uncontaminated wine these doctors started to produce their own vintages, with the primary aim of obtaining better quality wine to help their patients.

Left *Dr Thomas Fiaschi (1853–1927) of Sydney Hospital.*
Right *Dr Henry John Lindeman (1811–1881), Australias' first truly
commercial 'wine doctor' and founder of Lindemans Wines.*

## VARIOUS WINES

USED IN

## SICKNESS

AND

## CONVALESCENCE

Lecture to the Members of the Australasian Trained
Nurses' Association by Dr. Thomas Fiaschi
on June 27th, 1906

*Cover of the lecture paper given to nurses by Dr Fiaschi in 1906.*

Australia's early wine doctors wrote about the medicinal virtues of their wine. In 1871 Dr Lindeman wrote a letter to the N.S.W. Medical Gazette entitled 'Pure Wine as a Therapeutic Agent and Why it Should Become our National Beverage'. In 1906 Dr Thomas Fiaschi addressed the Australasian Trained Nurses' Association with a paper 'The Various Wines used in Sickness and Convalescence'. He stated: *'To avoid misunderstandings, I tell you frankly that I consider the temperate use of wine a valuable support to healthy man in this thorny path of life, and that the judicious use of it has proved itself to me of incalculable benefit in the treatment of the sick and convalescent'.*

Of all the vineyards established by medical vignerons in Australia, the most unusual were those established in the lunatic asylums in the nineteenth century. Asylums were rife with malnutrition and dysentery. One of the most common causes of insanity, other than tertiary syphilis, was contamination of home brewed alcohol by heavy metals causing heavy metal poisoning of the nervous system.

## PURE WINE AS A THERAPEUTIC AGENT, AND WHY IT SHOULD BECOME OUR NATIONAL BEVERAGE.

*(To the Editors of the Medical Gazette.)*

Sirs,—More than thirty years ago, when I first arrived in the colony, I was induced to plant the vine, and to impress upon my fellow-colonists the desirability of doing so likewise, seeing the great necessity there existed for supplying a pure exhilirating wine to take the place of ardent spirits and of adulterated wines and beers then and now the popular beverage of our community, the use of which frequently induces the diseases I have found mostly to be guarded against in our climate—namely, those arising from derangement of the liver ; to suffer from which too often robs life of enjoyment by enveloping it in a perpetual fog of mental depression, and for which depression relief is generally sought in the deleterious stimulants above-named, which invariably add fuel to fire, thereby crowding our community with the inebriate and insane.

It was natural to hope that a wise government would have seen the value of encouraging a step tending to scatter health and enjoyment, and to advance sobriety among the people it rules over by allowing this wine to be sold without any restrictions further than by demanding a small fee in the shape of a license from a vendor, sufficient to pay for the surveillance necessitated to be kept by the dishonest trader, who might otherwise for his profit adulterate it. But this has not yet been found the case. Several years ago a bill was introduced into the house by Mr. Holroyd with the view of getting this great boon conferred upon our community, but King Rum was found all too powerful, and his then influence upon electors, I believe, was the sole cause of its being rejected—I must not say rejected (it would have been well had it been so,) for it was passed in such a mutilated form as to appear a burlesque upon legislation, and to become a stumbling block, over which all future attempts have fallen. Sir, the advocacy of this cause I cannot but think should be taken up by the members of the medical profession, who are for the most part aware of the value of a pure wine as a therapeutic agent, and how materially we should benefit both in health and morals if it became our national beverage

I have spent many years of my life trying to bring this about by doing everything within my limited orbit to inculcate a taste for a pure, dry, and thoroughly fermented wine, free from excess of undecomposed sugar, and light in alcohol, resembling as much as possible the pure growths of Bordeaux and the Rheingan, and for the production of which our climate and soil are pre-eminently adapted.

To change a national taste in a life-time I never had the vanity to propose to myself, but to advance it somewhat is something to be proud of, and it will be a grand step gained to get the members of our profession to enlist themselves in this good cause, which, by bringing it prominently before them (with your permission) in the leaves of the *Medical Gazette,* I hope to do, knowing how great is the influence of the profession when stepping forward to advance mankind.

I have the honor to be, Sir,
Your obedient servant,

Sydney, June 12, 1871.                    W. T. LINDEMAN, M.R.C.S. Eng.

*A letter written by Dr Lindeman to the Medical Gazette 1871,*
*advocating the medicinal use of wine.*

*Because British prisons were over crowded, many convicts were imprisoned in old hulks. This is one is moored on the banks of the Thames, circa 1700s.*

Wine was championed by Australian doctors because it was a pure alternative to other forms of alcohol which were adulterated; and it treated malnutrition and dysentery. Tending the vineyard was also a form of outdoor work therapy for asylum patients.

Vineyards were established in Sydney at the Tarban Creek Asylum, by Dr Frederick Norton Manning and in South Australia at Parkside Asylum, by Dr William Lennox Cleland. In Victoria vineyards were established at the Ararat Asylum by Dr Beattie-Smith and at the Sunbury Asylum by Dr William Watkins.

More than 160 Australian vineyards have now been established by medical doctors. Some of the well known vineyards established in the 'modern era' include the boutique vineyards of Dr John Middleton's Mount Mary vineyard in the Yarra Valley, north of Melbourne in the mid 1950s and Dr Max Lake's, Lake's Folly vineyard in the Hunter Valley, north of Sydney in the mid 1960s.

Now every wine region in Australia, from Tasmania to Queensland and from Western Australia to New South Wales has a host of wine doctors. The Margaret River wine region to the south of Perth in Western Australia was founded by Perth cardiologist Dr Tom Cullity at his Vasse Felix vineyard. About half the vineyards there including Cullens, Moss Wood, Xanadu and Piero were established by medical doctors.

Wine is an integral part of the Australian medical profession's heritage. Rather than the traditional snake caduceus, the profession's symbol in Australia could well be a glass of wine and a set of convict leg irons!

## SUMMARY OF THE
## EARLY MEDICINAL USES OF WINE

1   As an antiseptic to purify water, to prevent dysentry and other bowel infections, to cleanse wounds and skin before operations.

2   As a sedative or tranquilizer.

3   As a hypnotic or sleeping medicine to sedate the patient.

4   Light white wines as anti-nauseants.

5   Appetite stimulants for convalescing patients.

6   Restorative tonics during convalescence through the vitamins, minerals, trace elements, protein, carbohydrates and sugar content.

7   Potent red wines such as port as anaemia treatments through their iron content.

8   As a diuretic.

9   As a purgative or to treat diarrhoea.

10  As a coolant, rubbed over patients' bodies to reduce fevers.

11  Mixed with other substances to draw out infection and foreign matter from wounds.

12  As the main mixing medium with less palatable medicines.

# | 3 |

# WINE:
# A MODERN MEDICINE

## CURRENT RESEARCH
## AND FINDINGS

### A PREVENTATIVE
### HEALTH MEASURE

The health benefits of wine are currently being scientifically explored in depth by leading researchers around the world. In Western society the two biggest disease groups are vascular disease, including heart attack and stroke and stress related disease, including anxiety, irritable bowel syndrome, tension headache, tension chest pain, palpitations, insomnia and nausea. According to the latest data from the Australian Bureau of Statistics, heart attacks and strokes alone, claim approximately 52 000 lives each year. Wine taken in moderation has been shown to help reduce the risk of both disease groups significantly.

Recent studies show that the death rate from vascular disease can be halved by consuming wine in moderation. Australia's annual death rate could possibly be reduced, by approximately 25 000. According to some studies, consuming wine in moderation reduces death from all causes in over 40-year olds by up to 50 per cent. After ceasing to smoke, consuming wine in moderation is a significant preventative health measure and will increase life expectancy. In fact, abstaining from moderate wine consumption is now accepted by the medical profession as being associated with an increase in vascular disease.

# KEY FINDINGS FROM LEADING STUDIES

Many studies carried out in the past decade demonstrate the health benefits of moderate wine consumption. Professor Charles Hennekens from Harvard University Medical School in the USA published the paper *'A Prospective Study of Moderate Alcohol Consumption and The Risk of Coronary Disease and Stroke in Women'* in the *New England Journal of Medicine* in 1988. The research found that: *'the prospective data suggest that among middle age women, moderate alcohol consumption decreases the risk of coronary heart disease and ischaemic stroke'*.

In 1991 Dr Eric Rimm, also from the Harvard University Medical School, published a paper *'Prospective Study of Alcohol Consumption and Risk of Coronary Heart Disease in Men'* in the British medical journal, *The Lancet* showing: *'these findings support the hypothesis that the inverse relation between alcohol consumption and risk of heart disease is causal'*. That is, alcohol consumption lowers the risk of heart attack.

Also in 1991 Dr Rodney Jackson, an epidemiologist from the University of Auckland, came to a similar conclusion in his paper *'Alcohol Consumption and Risk of Coronary Heart Disease'* published in the *British Medical Journal* stating: *'the results support the hypothesis that light to moderate alcohol consumption reduces the risk of coronary heart disease'*.

The world's leading epidemiologist, Sir Richard Doll from Oxford University Medical School in Britain published the paper *'Mortality in Relation to Consumption of Alcohol: 13 Years of Observations on Male British Doctors'* in the *British Medical Journal* in 1994. He concluded: *'among British men in middle or older age the consumption of an average of one or two units of alcohol a day is associated with significantly lower all cause mortality than is the consumption of no alcohol, or the consumption of substantial amounts'*.

Professor Serge Renaud's famous 'French Paradox' paper *'Wine, Alcohol, Platelets and the French Paradox for Coronary Heart Disease'*, published in *The Lancet* in 1992, placed wine and health on centre stage. The paper concluded: *'wine is the most effective drug yet discovered for the prevention of heart disease'*.

The paper's findings were reported by *60 Minutes* in the USA, wine sales surged as a result.

# THE FRENCH PARADOX

The 'French Paradox' is a term coined by Professor Serge Renaud, an epidemiologist at the University of Bordeaux, during research into wine consumption and heart disease. The strong link between the consumption of saturated fat and mortality by coronary heart disease is undisputed. In France however, where the national diet is high in saturated fat and the consumption of wine is the highest of any country, the incidence of heart disease is significantly lower than in northern Europe and the USA. This is now known as the 'French Paradox'.

Population studies of alcohol consumption and the incidence of heart disease have shown that moderate consumption of alcohol reduces the risk of coronary heart disease but high consumption or no consumption increases the risk of heart disease.

*Dr Serge Renaud, coined the term 'French Paradox'.*

# NOT ALL ALCOHOL IS EQUAL: WINE, BEER OR SPIRITS, DOES IT MATTER?

The comprehensive Copenhagen Heart Study proves that wine over any other form of alcohol provides health benefits. *'Mortality Associated with Moderate Intakes of Wine, Beer or Spirits'*, the study by Dr Morten Gronbaek of the Danish Epidemiology Science Centre, Institute of Preventive Medicine, Copenhagen Hospital Corporation in Denmark, known as *'The Copenhagen Heart Study'*, was published in the *British Medical Journal* in 1995. It was the first study to separate alcohol consumers into wine, beer and spirits drinkers.

In the study 6051 men and 7234 women, aged between 30 and 70 years, were studied over 10 to 12 years from 1976 to 1988, comparing their death rates and causes.

The researchers found: *'Low to moderate intake of wine is associated with lower mortality from cardiovascular and cerebrovascular disease and other causes. Similar intake of spirits implied an increased risk, while beer drinking did not affect mortality'*.

# THE COPENHAGEN HEART STUDY: A TURNING POINT IN THINKING

This study revealed that moderate wine consumers reduced their cardiovascular — heart attack — and cerebrovascular — stroke —- death rates, as well as death from all other causes by up to 50 per cent. The mortality rate of moderate beer drinkers was not affected, but the death rate of moderate spirits drinkers increased by 34 per cent.

A study published in 1998 by Professor Serge Renaud showed similar results, proving conclusively that consuming wine in moderation on a regular basis is healthy and sensible. In his paper *'Alcohol and mortality in middle-aged men from Eastern France'* he wrote: *'We conclude that a moderate intake of alcohol, mostly in the form of wine, seems to protect from death, not only from CHD (coronary heart disease) and cardiovascular diseases in general, but also from other causes. The results of the present prospective study, the first in France of the benefits of moderate wine drinking, appear to confirm the speculation that the so-called 'French Paradox' is due, at least in part, to the regular consumption of wine'*.

# WHAT IS ALCOHOL?

Alcohol is a compound made up of carbon, hydrogen and oxygen. There are many different types of alcohol depending on the number of carbon atoms in the chain, but the one that concerns us in this discussion is ethyl alcohol or ethanol, which is the result of fermentation of the sugars from fruits, berries and grains resulting in wine, cider, beer and spirits.

# WHAT'S IN IT?
# THE KEY CONSTITUENTS OF WINE

Wine is a complex liquid food made up of many substances which vary from bottle to bottle. Each wine differs according to the grape varieties used to make the wine; the soil type, climate and aspect of the vineyard supplying the grapes; the winemaking techniques and types of maturation — in oak or stainless steel — used before bottling.

The main components of wine are: WATER, which accounts for up to 90 per cent of wine by volume; ALCOHOL, mainly in the form of ethyl alcohol or ethanol, accounting for up to 20 per cent of wine by volume, most wines have an alcohol content of between 10 per cent and 14 per cent; SUGAR, mainly as glucose and fructose, the sweeter the wine the higher the sugar content; and ACIDS such as tartaric acid, malic acid, citric acid and acetic acid in very small amounts.

Another component of wine are the phenolic bioflavonoid compounds which form ANTIOXIDANTS. This is one source of the health benefits of wine, separating it from other forms of alcohol which do not contain these antioxidants.

Wine also contains various VITAMINS, MINERALS, TRACE ELEMENTS and AMINO ACIDS, the building blocks of protein, adding to its health and longevity benefits.

# HOW MUCH IS SAFE?

In exploring the medicinal virtues of wine in moderation we must define the term moderation. The Australian National Health and Medical Research Council's guidelines for safe drinking recommend a maximum of four standard drinks per day for an adult male and a maximum of two standard drinks per day for an adult female.

The recommended wine consumption for women is less than the amount recommended for men as women are generally smaller and have a relatively higher fat to muscle ratio. Because alcohol is lipophobic, that is, it prefers to go to tissues other than fat and women's bodies contain half the amount of alcohol dehydrogenase, the enzyme which metabolises alcohol, they are unable to process alcohol as efficiently as men.

## A STANDARD DRINK FOR MEN AND WOMEN

A standard drink is defined in Australia as the equivalent of 10 gms of alcohol or approximately 120–150 mls of wine, depending on the strength of the wine. It is a measure of alcohol designed to work out safe drinking levels.

| Spirits | Port/Sherry | Wine | Full Strength Beer | Light Beer |
|---------|-------------|------|--------------------|------------|
| 1 nip | 1 glass | 1 glass | 1 medium glass | 1 large glass |
| 30mls | 60mls | 120mls | 285mls | 425mls |
| 40% alcohol | 20% alcohol | 12% alcohol | 4.9% alcohol | 2.7% alcohol |

*These drinks are all standard servings throughout Australia.*
*They contain different volumes and concentrations of alcohol.*
*Each one is a 'standard drink' because it contains 10 grams of alcohol.*

## WHO SHOULDN'T DRINK:
## ALCOHOL ABUSE

It must be emphasised that these safe drinking levels apply only to moderate amounts of alcohol, consumed on a regular daily basis, rather than consumed at one time. Binge drinking — consuming a large quantity of alcohol in one sitting — is very harmful.

Many people think of alcoholics as people who drink too much alcohol on a regular daily basis, however binge drinkers are alcoholics as well, because they are allowing excessive amounts of alcohol to damage their health. Binge drinkers are often the hardest to convince that they have a severe drinking problem because of the misconception that an alcoholic requires a daily 'fix'. This is not the case.

Excluded from these safe drinking recommendations is anyone with a pre-existing disease which could be adversely affected by alcohol, such as a disease of the stomach eg ulcers; liver eg cirrhosis; pancreas eg pancreatitis; nervous system eg neuropathy; and heart eg myocarditis, myocardopathy or diseased heart muscle.

Safe drinking levels also apply only to mature adults and do not include under-age drinkers, who can seriously damage their health by consuming alcohol.

Abuse of alcohol also severely damages nerve cells, leading to brain damage eg Wernicke's encephalopathy, Korsakoff's syndrome and peripheral neuropathy — altered sensation of feel and other forms of nerve degeneration.

## THE PATTERN OF DRINKING IS IMPORTANT

When discussing the health benefits of consuming wine it is important to consider the manner in which wine is consumed, compared with the way in which other forms of alcohol are consumed. There is evidence to suggest the health benefits of wine are due in part to its alcohol content. The alcohol in wine lowers the bad cholesterol, increases the good cholesterol and acts as an anticoagulant or anti blood-clotting agent, thinning the blood and helping to reduce vascular disease.

Other medical scientists believe wine's benefit is also due to its high antioxidant content, which beer and spirits lack.

The antioxidants in wine reduce the amount of bad cholesterol or low density lipoprotein (LDL) deposited in blood vessel walls, help prevent cancer and reduce the effects of ageing and degenerative diseases.

Another group of scientists believe that the way in which we consume wine is the key issue. Because wine is usually consumed by sipping slowly during a meal, it is therefore absorbed more slowly over a longer period of time. In association with food, the absorption rate of the alcohol component in the wine is far less than when consuming beer or spirits, which are usually drunk on an empty stomach.

Consuming food while drinking wine does two things. First, it significantly slows down the stomach's emptying time. Because it is busy digesting the food, alcohol is passed into the rest of the digestive system more slowly, to be absorbed into the blood stream later. Second, it allows the consumer to gain the health benefits of the food that they are consuming. A symptom of alcoholism is poor nutrition and a lack of vitamin B1 thiamine hydrochloride, which can result in dementia, amongst other things.

The manner in which wine is consumed is certainly very significant in its health benefits. Wine in moderation is healthy because of a combination of: the alcohol component benefit, combined with the antioxidant component benefit plus the mode of consumption benefit.

## THE BENEFITS OF WINE CONSUMPTION: A GLOBAL CONCLUSION

We are entering a new 'wine age', with wine forming the basis of a healthy lifestyle. As the world's societies continue to advance and we strive to attain a theoretical optimum life span of 120 years, the most common causes of death are moving from infections and malnutrition, still widespread in less developed societies, to vascular disease, cancer and degenerative disease now prevalent in well developed societies.

Prevention of the more advanced diseases, rather than treatment through bypass surgery, cancer surgery, radiotherapy and chemotherapy will become increasingly important as we endeavour to improve both quality and quantity of life.

Consuming wine in moderation will play a leading role in this new age of healthier and happier people. As pointed out previously, it is more realistic to entice the general population to consume wine in moderation with meals than it is to persuade them to participate in other preventative health measures such as stopping smoking, reducing weight, increasing exercise, lowering blood pressure, cholesterol and sugar intake.

Studies carried out around the world, involving men and women from different societies, have shown that the health benefits of wine are universal and not restricted to one group. Thus wine, consumed in moderation daily, should become the universal health drink and preventative medicine.

The following studies of different population groups in different countries have all reached the same conclusions on the positive effects of moderate alcohol consumption, including wine. They find that moderate consumers of alcohol have lower death rates than abstainers or heavy drinkers. These studies include the work of Professor Charles Hennekens, Professor of Medicine at Harvard University (USA); Dr Eric Rimm, epidemiologist at Harvard University (USA); Dr Klatsky, senior consultant cardiologist, Kaiser Permanente Medical Centre, Oakland, California (USA); Dr Rodney Jackson, epidemiologist at the University of Auckland (NZ); Dr Kevin Cullen, physician in charge of the Busselton Study (Australia); Dr Simon de Burgh, School of Public Health, University of Sydney (Australia); Dr Serge Renaud, epidemiologist at the University of Bordeaux (France); Dr Michael Marmot, Professor of Epidemiology and Public Health, University College London (UK); Professor Morten Gronbaek, epidemiologist, University of Copenhagen (Denmark); and Professor Leon Simons, Professor of Medicine, University of NSW (Australia). All have shown through scientific research that wine is beneficial to health.

Another study in Japan which compared coronary angiograms — X-rays of the heart's arteries — of teetotallers, moderate drinkers and heavy drinkers showed the moderate drinkers to have the least diseased coronary angiograms.

The World's leading epidemiologist and Emeritus Regius Professor of Medicine at Oxford University, Sir Richard Doll, believes the positive effect of alcohol, including wine, in moderation has been conclusively demonstrated. Abstainers and heavy drinkers have a higher incidence of disease than do moderate drinkers, he found. This U-shaped relationship between alcohol and disease, he believes is irrefutable. *'When we allow for age, smoking and other known risk factors, the moderate drinkers have the lowest total death rates and the lowest rates for vascular deaths'*, he writes.

In 1997 Sir Richard Doll published in the *British Medical Journal* the result of his research into alcohol and health, as well as a review of all similar research work, *'One for the Heart'*. He concluded that even after you allow for the consequences of alcohol abuse, there remains a net health benefit for society in the consumption of alcohol, and recommended that public health policy makers should re-evaluate their anti-alcohol views accordingly.

*Sir Richard Doll*

# | 4 |

# WINE AND
# GOOD HEALTH

## HOW WINE CAN HELP
## YOU LEAD A HEALTHY LIFE

## WINE AND MOOD:
## THE PSYCHOLOGY OF DRINKERS
## AND ABSTAINERS

It has been well documented that heavy drinkers or abusers of alcohol have a high level of mood and anxiety disorders. However, little is known about the relationship between alcohol consumption and anxiety across the full spectrum of drinking behaviour — from abstinence to abuse. A recent study by Dr Brian Rodgers of the National Health and Medical Research Council (NHMRC), Psychiatric Epidemiology Research Centre in Canberra, Australia, has shown that there is a U-shaped relationship between depression and the level of alcohol consumption, suggesting that abstainers, as well as heavy drinkers, are at an increased risk of mood and anxiety disorders. According to the study, moderate consumers of alcohol are the more mentally balanced group.

Wine is often served before and during evening meals to boost the spirit and morale, stimulate the appetite and aid digestion. This is an important use of wine among convalescent patients in hospitals and nursing homes because it has been shown to speed up recovery. This is an obvious health benefit, and also benefits society in reducing hospital expenses.

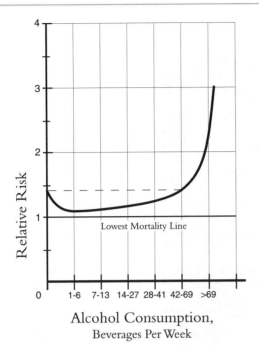

Alcohol Consumption,
Beverages Per Week

*Relative risk of mortality in relation to alcohol intake. Risk is set at 1.00 for lowest mortality. Moderate drinkers have a lower mortality risk than abstainers and heavy drinkers. (After Dr M. Gronbaek)*

## RELAX!
## LIVE HAPPILY AND LONGER:
## WINE USED TO
## CONTROL STRESS AND
## REDUCE BLOOD PRESSURE

Stress related disease is increasingly prevalent in our society. The common irritable bowel syndrome, in which the bowel responds poorly to stress with abdominal cramping, alternating diarrhoea and constipation and the passing of flatus or wind in large amounts, accounts for up to half of all gastrointestinal symptoms. Other stress related conditions include anxiety, palpitations, tension headaches, tension chest pains, which may often be confused with heart attack pains, insomnia, nausea, hyperventilation and dizziness.

# THE ARTERY DISEASE PROCESS

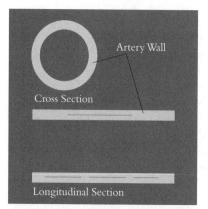

*Normal coronary artery.*

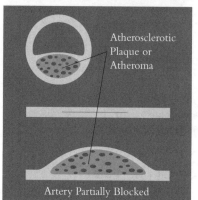

*As age increases, atherosclerotic plaque or atheroma, accumulates within the artery wall and blood supply is reduced. This can cause angina if the artery goes to the heart, transient ischemic attack if the artery goes to the brain or peripheral vascular disease if the artery goes to the lower limbs.*

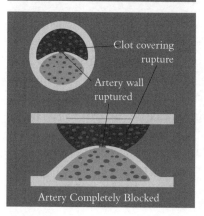

*With further increase in age, the atheroma continues to accumulate within the artery wall. It reaches a point where it ruptures the internal artery wall and a clot forms to cover the rupture. The artery is now completely blocked, resulting in a heart attack if the artery goes to the heart, a stroke if the artery goes to the brain or gangrene if the artery goes to the lower limbs, due to death of the tissue no longer supplied with blood by the artery.*

As a doctor I encourage patients to assess the cause of their stress and to resolve the problem or learn to cope by using some form of relaxation therapy. Patients often require a form of adjunct therapy, so I recommend a glass or two of wine at the end of a stressful day. This relaxes the patient as effectively as any anti-anxiety pill such as the benzodiazepams, Valium or Serapax. In addition, wine serves as a form of food and good preventative medicine. Wine consumed in the evening also helps patients to sleep and may eliminate the necessity of a sleeping pill. Wine in moderation, therefore, is a good substitute for many prescription drugs.

Heavy alcohol consumption raises blood pressure but Dr Rodney Jackson, an epidemiologist from Auckland University, showed in 1985 that moderate drinkers 'have either similar or lower blood pressure levels compared to non drinkers'. This could be due to the fact that alcohol in moderation acts as a relaxant, dilates blood vessels, and acts as an anticoagulant reducing blood viscosity or thickness, which lowers blood pressure.

## VASCULAR DISEASE: THE ROLE OF WINE IN ITS PREVENTION

The biggest killer in Western society is vascular disease, which accounts for half of the deaths in most advanced countries. It occurs either as coronary heart disease — heart attacks — as ischaemic cerebrovascular accidents — strokes — as aortic aneurysms — swelling of the aorta, the main artery in the body — as deep vein thrombosis — clots in the legs — or as peripheral vascular disease.

## WHY DO HEART ATTACKS HAPPEN?

Vascular disease in the form of heart attack or stroke occurs when blood vessels become blocked; when too much fat in the form of low density lipoprotein (LDL) or 'bad cholesterol' becomes deposited within the blood vessel wall. Eventually this fat, called atherosclerotic plaque, swells up and forms an obstruction to blood flow. By altering blood flow, this fatty plaque can also cause the blood to clot.

Or, the fat can swell up to the point where it bursts through the internal lining of the artery wall, causing a clot to form to breach the tear in the wall of the artery. Whatever the mechanism, when a blood vessel becomes blocked, it causes death to the tissue the blood vessel supplies, resulting in a heart attack or stroke.

# WHAT IS CHOLESTEROL?

Cholesterol is an organic substance belonging to the steroid family which circulates in the blood stream. It is a white, waxy, odourless and tasteless substance that has several essential functions to sustain life in animals and humans. First, it is one of the primary components of the membrane that forms the cell wall. Second, it is the compound from which the body makes bile acids to help the bowel digest fats and vitamin D to help form bones and steroid hormones.

Cholesterol is made by the liver and ingested in the diet in the form of animal fats. It is possible to be on a low cholesterol diet, but still have a high blood cholesterol level through inheriting a liver prone to making excessive amounts of cholesterol, such as in familial hyperlipidogenia.

Cholesterol is carried around in the blood by substances called lipoproteins because it is insoluble in blood. Low density lipoprotein (LDL) transports cholesterol from the liver, where it is made or stored from the diet, out to the tissues where it is needed. Excessive amounts of cholesterol can be deposited in blood vessel walls, causing obstructive atheromatous plaques.

High density lipoprotein (HDL) does the opposite and transports cholesterol back from the tissues to the liver to be metabolised or converted to bile salts and then excreted via the bowel. Thus high HDL levels are good, because they help lower damaging cholesterol levels in the tissues.

## HOW TO AVOID A HEART ATTACK

Wine significantly reduces vascular disease — especially heart attack, stroke and deep vein thrombosis. Some studies have shown this reduction can be as high as 50 per cent. It does this by raising the HDL or High Density Lipoprotein — the good cholesterol — which clears away atheroma or the plaque which blocks arteries.

Wine also reduces LDL or Low Density Lipoprotein — the bad cholesterol — which initially forms the atheroma. While these are long-term effects, wine in moderation also has a short-term 24-hour effect by acting as an anti-coagulant or anti-blood clotting agent, reducing clot or thombus formation. These clots can break off and embolize, blocking the artery further downstream and possibly causing a complete obstruction of the artery resulting in a heart attack, or they can form when atheromatous plaque ruptures.

A moderate daily dose of wine will help prevent stroke or heart attack.

Another vascular benefit of wine has been shown in a study from America in 1997, where moderate drinkers were shown to have half the rate of DVT — Deep Vein Thrombosis, or clot in the leg — to that of teetotallers.

## SUMMARY OF BENEFICIAL EFFECTS
## OF WINE ON VASCULAR DISEASE

1   Increases good cholesterol (HDL), which clears away atheromatous plaque.

2   Decreases bad cholesterol (LDL) which forms atheromatous plaque.

3   Is an anticoagulant, so thins the blood to prevent clots from forming.

4   Contains the antioxidants resveratrol, quercetin and epicatechin which prevent LDL from entering the artery wall to form atheromatous plaque.

5   Reduces stress by acting as a relaxant.

# POSITIVE EFFECTS ON BLOOD FLOW AND THE HEALTH OF THE ELDERLY

The blood flow, or tissue perfusion, in a moderate drinker is better than in a teetotaller or heavy drinker, so a moderate wine drinker gains other vascular benefits besides fewer heart attacks. Better blood flow through bones leads to a reduction in osteoporosis, or thinning of the bones with age.

A study from the University of California by Professor Holbrook in 1993 showed that moderate drinkers have stronger bones.

In addition, better blood flow to the brain has been shown to have a positive effect on intellect in people over 65-years of age. In 1993 Professor Jean-March Orgogozo, Professor of Neurology and Professor Jean-Francois Dartigues, Professor of Epidemiology from Bordeaux University, showed that moderate drinkers in the study averaged better than non drinkers in tests measuring intelligence. In a 1997 paper they also demonstrated that moderate drinkers had less dementia and Alzheimer's disease. A similar result was shown in a 1993 study in Indiana, USA, with veterans over 65-years of age.

# WINE AND THE INCIDENCE OF STROKE

It is claimed by the anti-alcohol lobby that the incidence of stroke is increased with alcohol consumption. This is true for haemorrhagic strokes, where a swelling in one of the brain's arteries, called an aneurysm bursts and bleeds, damaging the surrounding brain tissue. Because of the anti-coagulant effect of alcohol in thinning the blood it makes the haemorrhage worse.

Haemorrhagic strokes, however, account for only five per cent of strokes. Up to 95 per cent of strokes are ischaemic strokes, where the brain's arteries gradually block off with atheroma, just as the coronary arteries can, leading to heart attacks. Consuming wine in moderation brings about a clear health benefit by preventing ischaemic strokes as a result of modifying atheromatous plaques.

## CAN WINE HELP TO PREVENT CANCER?

Professor Serge Renaud in his latest paper *'Alcohol and Mortality in Middle-Aged Men From Eastern France'* published in *Epidemiology* in 1998 showed a 24 per cent reduction in cancer rates, in general, in men who drank wine in moderation.

Researchers at the CSIRO Division of Human Nutrition in Adelaide, Australia have been conducting experiments on the effects of the antioxidant content in wine on cancer. Excessive consumption of alcohol may induce cancer formation, especially in the digestive system, but in moderation the antioxidants in red and white wine were shown to have significant potential for reducing oxidative damage to DNA, the main building blocks for chromosomes or genetic material. Damaged DNA causes the formation of abnormal genes, leading to abnormal cells and cancer.

The work of Professor John Pezzuto of the University of Illinois, USA on the antioxidant resveratrol in wine has shown that resveratrol prevents cells from turning cancerous and slows down the spread of malignant cells.

The key, then, to wine's anti-cancer action is its antioxidant content. Wine must be consumed in moderate doses only, as an excess of alcohol can actually have the adverse effect of causing cancer.

## A SOURCE OF ANTIOXIDANTS

The latest research into the health benefits of wine has focused on the role of various antioxidants in wine, including the bioflavonoids resveratrol, quercetin and epicatechin, which inhibit LDL or low density lipoprotein — bad cholesterol — from oxidising.

LDL must be oxidised before it can be stored in vessel walls to form atheroma, which can lead to blockage of arteries and subsequent heart attack or stroke. Having antioxidants present in blood prevents this from happening. Antioxidants also neutralise the effects of the body's harmful metabolic waste products called free radicals, rogue molecules with an extra, unpaired, electron.

Free radicals cause biochemical havoc in the body by hindering normal biochemical pathway function, resulting in degenerative diseases such as premature aging, cancer and vascular disease.

The best known antioxidants are vitamins C and E, but the most potent antioxidants occur in wine. Dr Edwin N Frankel at Davis University in California has shown that antioxidants contained in wine are five times stronger than vitamin E, achieving 100 per cent antioxidant activity in the blood, whereas vitamin E plateaus at only 20 per cent antioxidant activity or effect.

Wine contains more antioxidants than any other alcoholic beverage. In addition, a glass of wine is a more pleasant accompaniment to a meal than a vitamin E capsule.

New research by Professor John Pezzuto at the University of Illinois has shown that the antioxidant resveratrol also prevents human body cells from turning cancerous and inhibits the spread of cells that are already malignant.

This has been supported by Dr Serge Renaud's latest research which has demonstrated a 24 per cent reduction in death rates from cancer in moderate wine consumers. The exciting new research into resveratrol shows that it has other benefits, as well as its antioxidant role, in reducing vascular disease, cancer and other illnesses.

Scientists at the University of Milan have shown that resveratrol stimulates M.A.P. kinase, which is an enzyme that can assist nerve cells to regenerate. This may help to explain why wine drinkers have less neuro-degenerative diseases such as Alzheimer's disease, the commonest cause of dementia and Parkinson's disease. Resveratrol in wine helps nerve cells in the brain grow extensions, which enable them to connect to neighbouring nerve cells. When neurodegenerative diseases occur these connections break down. Dr Bertelli, head of the research group said that *by daily reinforcing these contacts we can prevent neurodegeneration*.

By consuming wine in moderation the vascular tree within the brain is less likely to become diseased by atheroma formation and clotting, so it is able to supply brain nerves with more blood containing essential oxygen and glucose. This is another mechanism by which wine helps the brain function better.

Wine taken in moderation could be referred to as brain food or brain friendly, as studies have shown it prevents strokes and nerve cell degeneration. This is in marked contrast to what was previously thought, about the effects of any form of alcohol on the brain.

Dr Kindl at the University of Marburg in Germany has isolated the genes for the synthesis of resveratrol in grapevine DNA, enabling these genes to be incorporated into new wine root stock. Making resveratrol enriched wine from this root stock opens up a new era in preventative health, with the possibility of taking a daily dose of resveratrol enriched wine.

## WINE AND DIABETICS

The only substance that does not have any caloric value is water. Diabetics have a raised blood sugar level, making it necessary to watch and control their caloric intake. Dry wines have had all their sugar converted to alcohol, leaving no free sugar in them, but dry wines still have caloric value. Diabetics can drink dry wines but need to include the wine's caloric value in their daily diet caloric count. Other forms of alcohol, namely beer and spirits have a much higher caloric value than dry wines and should be avoided by diabetics.

## HOW WINE HELPS TO PREVENT GALLSTONES

Moderate wine consumption significantly reduces the rate of gall-stone formation by dissolving cholesterol. Gallstones are formed by bile salts accumulating on a nucleus of dead bacterium in the gallbladder. Cholesterol forms the bile salts which the body uses to emulsify and breakdown fat in the diet. Wine consumed in moderation reduces bad cholesterol levels, bile salts and so the rate of gallstone formation.

Wine also speeds up the emptying and filling of the gallbladder with bile salts. The increase in bile flow means there is less stagnation of the bile and this effect, coupled with a reduced cholesterol level has been thought to explain why wine drinkers have up to 40 per cent fewer gallstones than abstainers.

## WINE AND
## LIVER DISEASE

Until recently it was thought that all alcohol consumption contributed to liver disease. It has now been shown that consuming alcohol in moderation does not cause liver disease such as cirrhosis, which is caused by alcohol abuse. These breakthrough studies, carried out in Italy and Denmark indicate that only for those drinking more than 70 units of alcohol per week, a minority of about five per cent, would develop liver disease. The UK Government recommends a limit of 21 units of alcohol a week for men and 14 units for women.

## PREVENTING
## STOMACH ULCERS

A German study published in the *British Medical Journal* in 1997 has shown that one or two alcoholic drinks a day could protect people against Helicobacter Pylori infection. Helicobacter Pylori is the bacterium which is associated with causing stomach ulcers. The antiseptic properties in alcohol are responsible for this effect. So moderate consumers of alcohol, including wine, should have fewer ulcers caused by Helicobacter Pylori. A 1997 Harvard study found that moderate alcohol consumers had significantly fewer duodenal ulcers, up to 53 per cent, than abstainers.

## AGEING WELL
## WITH WINE

Leon Simons, Professor of Medicine at the University of NSW, specialises in blood lipid or fat diseases at Sydney's St Vincent's Hospital. He began studying the causes of death of those aged 60 and over in Dubbo in 1988. The seven-year follow up study made two remarkable findings. Firstly, there are three things that significantly increase the risk of cardio vascular disease and rate of death in the elderly; diabetes, smoking and hypertension. Secondly, the only factor that significantly reduced the death rate was drinking in moderation. It reduced the death rate by up to 51 per cent in both men and women.

Professor Simons concluded: *'Alcohol intake in the Dubbo elderly appears to be independently associated with a significant increase in life expectancy'*.

Therfore unless there is a contraindication, drinking in moderation is the single most important preventative health measure one can take, besides not smoking.

## SEEING CLEARLY

Macular degeneration is a condition where the sensitive part of the eye's retina, enabling the eye to focus on objects, degenerates and dies off. Along with glaucoma, diabetes and hypertension, it is one of the main causes of blindness in our society. But unlike the other three causes there is no treatment for macular degeneration and once developed it gradually causes blindness. Researchers at the Howard University in Washington DC, USA in a paper published in 1998 showed that moderate wine consumers aged 45–75 had 20 per cent less aged macular degeneration than teetotallers, beer drinkers and spirits drinkers, due to wine's anti-coagulant and antioxidant effects.

# SUMMARY OF THE CURRENT
# MEDICAL BENEFITS OF WINE

1 Reduces vascular disease, due to improved blood flow, resulting in:
Reduced coronary heart disease
Reduced ischaemic stroke
Reduced deep vein thrombosis
Reduced osteoporosis
Increased intellect in the elderly
Reduced macular degeneration of the eye.

2 Is a tonic — contains most vitamins, minerals and trace elements.

3 Is a fat and cholesterol-free source of carbohydrate.

4 Reduces blood pressure.

5 Is an antiseptic due to the alcohol and polyphenols.

6 Increases morale and appetite, especially in nursing home and hospital patients.

7 Contains quercetin, resveratrol and epicatechin, potent antioxidants which have anti-carcinogen activity.

8 Potential to reduce colds due to antioxidant content.

9 Dry white wine is an alcoholic drink which may be suitable for diabetics.

10 Reduces gallstones.

# | 5 |

# RED WINE
# VERSUS
# WHITE WINE

Since Professor Serge Renaud's 'French Paradox' paper was published in *The Lancet* in 1991, wine consumers have had a mind-set that only red wine is good for them.

The 'French Paradox' refers to the observation that the French have significantly less coronary heart disease than in other comparable countries, despite a diet high in cholesterol predisposing them to vascular disease.

The reason for relatively low rates of coronary heart disease in France, according to Professor Renaud, is because the French are high consumers of wine.

## IS THERE A DIFFERENCE IN
## HEALTH BENEFITS?

Research now shows that whether wine is red or white does not matter.

So long as wine is consumed in moderation, on a regular basis, significant health benefits can be obtained. Death rates from all causes can be reduced by up to 50 per cent, by reducing vascular disease up to 50 per cent and cancer rates by up to 24 per cent. It also relieves societies other significant disease group, stress related diseases such as anxiety, tension headaches and pains, indigestion and palpitations.

Consuming red or white wine in moderation reduces levels of low density lipoprotein (LDL) or bad cholesterol and increases levels of high density lipoprotein (HDL) or good cholesterol in blood. Vascular disease occurs when bad cholesterol is deposited into artery walls, forming 'atheromatous plaques' which swell up over time. They eventually rupture causing a clot to form, blocking the artery and denying blood to the tissue supplied by that artery. Without blood the surrounding tissue dies.

High levels of good cholesterol are desirable because good cholesterol has the very beneficial effect of removing bad cholesterol from atheromatous plaques in artery walls, taking it back to the liver to be remetabolised.

Wine also acts as an anti-blood clotting agent or anti-coagulant, reducing the possibility of clot formation, further lowering the possibility of vascular disease.

# WHAT IS IN RED AND WHITE WINE?

Red and white wine contain important beneficial substances known as antioxidants. Antioxidants inhibit bad cholesterol from being incorporated into the artery wall and damage caused by free radicals. Free radicals are toxic waste products, formed in the body after bio-chemical interactions. They contribute to the  causation of degenerative diseases such as cancer, Alzheimer's disease, Parkinson's disease and ageing.

Red and white wine contain the three strongest antioxidants in nature called resveratrol, quercitin and epicatechin. They are five times stronger than vitamin C and E, the benchmarks for antioxidants.

Dr E. N. Frankel has shown that no matter how much vitamin C or E is taken, antioxidant activity, for a given level of oxides, plateaus at 20 per cent. Antioxidants in wine will plateau at 100 per cent after 2–3 glasses, ie the antioxidants in wine are five times more effective than those in vitamin C and E.

It should be noted that it is the fermentation process that converts grape juice into wine and produces alcohol. This process enhances antioxidant levels in wine many times and is why wine has far superior health benefits, compared to taking concentrated grape extract, as has been advocated by some in the anti-alcohol lobby.

Dr Frankel's research has also shown that red wine contains more antioxidants than white wine. The amount of antioxidant contained varies according to the grape variety, region, vintage climate — summer rainfall increases resveratrol levels because grapes produce more resveratrol in their skins as protection against fungus caused by moisture — soil, whether stored in oak — oaked wines have more antioxidants that unoaked wines — and filtration techniques.

Studies by Professor Geoff Skurray at the University of Western Sydney of filtration techniques has shown, for example, that the fining agent polyclar can remove 92 per cent of resveratrol, while casein, egg white and alginate also removed some resveratrol, but gelatin had relatively little effect.

The relevance of these laboratory findings for the wine drinker emerge when they are tested in population studies which compare red and white wine consumption and mortality.

There have been several recent studies which show that it doesn't matter.

In 1995 Vinson and Hontz from the Department of Chemistry at the University of Scranton published a paper titled *'Phenol Antioxidant Index: Comparative Antioxidant Effectiveness of Red and White Wines'*. This study showed that even though red wines had a higher phenol content than white wines, *'the white wines had a significantly lower IC50 (the concentration for 50% inhibition of low density lipoprotein or bad cholesterol) and thus were better antioxidants that red wines'*.

The important message from this study is that it does not matter what the total antioxidant or phenol levels are in a wine, but how effective are those antioxidants at doing their job. For inhibiting bad cholesterol, the antioxidants in white wines are shown to be more effective.

Dr. Karl Jung and associates at the University of Mainz published a paper in 1999 titled 'Moderate Red and White Wine Consumption and Risk of Cardiovascular Disease'. The paper concluded that, *'white and red wine improved the antioxidative capacity in the blood. The sum of the changes in cardiovascular protective blood values, the 'protective wine score', which includes all parameters, showed a clear improvement in both wine groups. The scores for moderate wine consumption were higher than for water, and white wine scored higher than red wine. Systolic blood pressure reduced significantly in the white wine group, and the diastolic blood pressure reduced in both wine groups. This study demonstrated that moderate regular wine consumption reduces the risk of cardiovascular disease. The effects of both German wines, red and white were comparable. In some parameters white wine delivered even better results than red wine'.*

In the United States research at the Jordan Heart Research Foundation found that free radicals were reduced by 15 per cent in red wine drinkers and by 34 per cent in white wine drinkers. Red wine drinkers experienced a 10 per cent reduction in blood clotting ability and white wine drinkers 20 per cent.

So why are the antioxidant molecules in white wine apparently more effective than those found in red wine even though they may be in greater number in red wine?

The answer lies in research undertaken by Dr Gordon Troup, a physicist at Monash University in Melbourne. Dr Troup examined the size of the antioxidant molecules in wine and showed that those in white wine are smaller than those in red wine. Because they are smaller, white wine antioxidant molecules can get further out into the tissues to do their job and are thus more effective than red wine antioxidant molecules.

In a letter to the International Journal of Food Science and Technology titled *'Free Radical Scavenging Abilities of Beverages'* Dr Troup et al wrote that *'...if the health-promoting properties of wines are related to their superoxide-scavenging abilities, then white wine is at least as effective as red'.*

The conclusion is that it does not matter which colour of wine, red or white, is consumed. Red and white wine contain alcohol and enough antioxidants to prevent vascular disease and reduce degenerative diseases.

What matters most is that the right wine is married to the right food. The best combination of wine and food is the most important criteria by which to choose a wine — not just because it is red!

# | 6 |

# THE ROLE
# OF WINE
# IN WOMEN'S
# HEALTH

Women's health issues of pregnancy, breastfeeding and breast cancer require special attention in the discussion of wine and health. Consuming wine during pregnancy or when breastfeeding is an issue that attracts conflicting advice.

Women, whether pregnant or breastfeeding or not, should keep within the recommended limit of a maximum of two standard drinks per day to avoid alcohol-related problems. If this limit is heeded, moderate consumption of wine should have no detrimental effect on a pregnant or lactating woman or on her baby.

The issue of safe drinking during pregnancy has been taken to the extreme in the USA, where by law wine bottles must carry a label with an official Government Health Warning which states that women should not consume alcohol while they are pregnant. It also warns against driving a car and operating machinery after drinking. The warning has been heeded to the extent that pregnant women have been refused wine in restaurants for fear of litigation were a baby to be born defective. According to research into the effects of alcohol on pregnant women and their babies, this is unnecessary if wine is consumed in moderation.

# FOETAL ALCOHOL SYNDROME

Foetal Alcohol Syndrome occurs in babies born to mothers who abused alcohol during their pregnancy. These babies are born with facial malformations and mental defects. A mother who limits herself to the safe drinking limits does not put her baby at risk of Foetal Alcohol Syndrome.

There is possibly a flaw in the American restauranteurs' thinking because most foetal damage occurs during the first trimester of pregnancy, when the pregnancy is not physically obvious. These women would be served alcohol, but the women who are obviously pregnant and in the second or third trimester, when there is less chance of Foetal Alcohol Syndrome because the baby is formed, would not be served alcohol.

I have seen patients who worry about the potential for Foetal Alcohol Syndrome, having consumed more than the safe limit of alcohol early on, before they were aware of their pregnancy. In all cases there was no ill-effect on their baby. A study by Dr Walpole in Western Australia found that most harm occurs due to the anxiety of pregnant women worrying about Foetal Alcohol Syndrome, rather than from moderate drinking during pregnancy.

It is possible that Foetal Alcohol Syndrome may have a multifactorial cause or pathogenesis, as most cases are from lower socioeconomic groups in large cities, so poor nutritional and pollution factors may also be involved.

Studies examined by the Royal College of Obstetricians and Gynaecologists in the UK have found that Foetal Alcohol Syndrome does not occur unless five or six drinks are consumed per day, regularly, by pregnant women. They have found no Foetal Alcohol Syndrome in babies of women who drink moderately. The Royal College of Obstetricians and Gynaecologists has a policy statement that consuming alcohol in moderation during pregnancy is safe.

A 1995 publication of The Department of Human Services and Health, *The Quantification of Drug Caused Morbidity & Mortality in Australia* concluded that there is no ill effect of light alcohol consumption — 10g of alcohol per day — on the foetus. The UK

Department of Health and The Royal College of Obstetricians and Gynaecologists reached the same conclusion in 1997.

The US Department of Agriculture, Health & Human Services in *Nutrition and your Health: Dietary Guidelines for Americans*, maintains that a safe level of alcohol consumption during pregnancy has not yet been established. The American health warning about pregnancy and drinking may be seen as a political statement to appease the anti-alcohol lobby. A medical statement based on medical fact would only advise women not to *abuse* alcohol during pregnancy.

## BREAST-FEEDING AND WINE CONSUMPTION

Women who are breastfeeding may drink wine in moderation safely, without harming their babies. Alcohol is secreted in breast milk but for a lactating woman who drinks wine in moderation, the amount of alcohol in her milk will be minimal; it will at worst make the baby a little sleepy. Lactating women who exceed the safe moderate level of wine consumption however, risk excessive bleeding in their babies due to the anti-coagulant effect of the alcohol.

## A LINK TO BREAST CANCER?

The risk of developing breast cancer has been linked both positively and negatively to the consumption of alcohol. Some studies have shown a slightly increased risk of developing breast cancer in drinkers while other studies have shown no increase or an actual reduction in the risk. If there is an increase, it is minimal and should be balanced against the proven vascular and other health benefits of consuming wine in moderation.

The question of a link between drinking wine and an increased risk of breast cancer remains unresolved, but it is currently believed that women are more likely to die from vascular disease, by abstaining from wine for instance, than from breast cancer, if they drink wine moderately.

In Australia about 2 500 women each year die from breast cancer but more than ten times this number die from vascular disease.

## PUBLIC POLICY ON WINE AND HEALTH AUSTRALIA

Because of the indisputable evidence about the health benefits of drinking wine in moderation, government and health industry bodies have had to rethink their conservative position on wine consumption. The new policy statement on alcohol by the Australian Medical Association acknowledges the health benefit of consuming wine: *'evidence suggests that not all patterns of alcohol use are harmful. Low levels of consumption reduce the risk from cardiovascular disease in older individuals'.*

## THE USA

The agency that governs nutritional and diet guidelines in the USA, the US Department of Health and Human Services, also states that consuming alcohol in moderation has a net health benefit.

*Nutrition and Health: Dietary Guidelines for Americans (1995)* defines moderation as *'no more than one drink per day for women, and no more than two drinks per day for men'*. This edition states: *'Alcoholic beverages have been used to enhance the enjoyment of meals by many societies throughout human history'*, and that *'current evidence suggests that moderate drinking is associated with a lower risk for coronary heart disease in some individuals'*.

Americans can now see a label on wine bottles touting the health benefits of drinking wine alongside the warning label. A voluntary label alluding to the positive aspects of drinking wine in moderation was approved in 1999.

This is in stark contrast to the official government position on alcohol taken early in the twentieth century. America had introduced 'prohibition' in 1919 and persisted with an anti-alcohol attitude long after the Prohibition Act had been repealed in 1933.

# THE UK

In its new safe drinking guidelines the UK Government's Health Department has increased the amount of alcohol one can safely consume. The most recent UK Department of Health report, *Sensible Drinking*, suggests a *'maximum health advantage of between one and two daily units'* where a unit is approximately one small glass of wine for both men and women, and acknowledges safe drinking levels of up to four units per day for men and three units per day for women.

The report states: *'It is now established that the main specific pathology which benefits from alcohol consumption is coronary heart disease'*, and that those people in the age group where there is significant risk of heart disease, who drink little, may wish *'to consider the possible benefits of light drinking'*.

# | 7 |

# CONCLUSION

## A LITTLE OF WHAT
## YOU FANCY
## DOES YOU GOOD

A large and authoritative pool of Australian and international evidence shows a net health benefit from consuming wine in moderation. Wine contains many substances including most amino acids, vitamins, minerals and trace elements, making it an excellent tonic. It is also a fat and cholesterol-free source of carbohydrate. Cardiologists around the world have heeded the new research, and many now consider being an abstainer from consuming wine in moderation is a risk factor in the development of vascular disease.

Our society should be aware of the harm as well as the benefits of alcohol, recognising those at particular risk of alcohol abuse. As Paracelsus said in the 16th century, *'Whether wine is a nourishment, medicine or poison is a matter of dosage'*.

In wine we have a 'medicine' capable of lowering morbidity and mortality in a much more palatable form than conventional medications. As a preventative vascular health tool, wine consumed in moderation is often an easier and more appealing alternative, as well as an adjunct, to conventional recommendations of exercise, weight loss, reducing cholesterol by dieting, reducing sugar intake, stopping smoking or taking cholesterol or blood pressure lowering pills.

The views of Dr Curtis Ellison, an epidemiologist from Boston

*Dr Curtis Ellison*

University and author of the American Council on Science and Health publication *Does Moderate Alcohol Consumption Prolong Life?* are worth considering. In it he writes: *'Through the ages conventional wisdom has been that the moderate intake of alcoholic beverages is consistent with a long and healthy life. Data from epidemiological studies within recent decades demonstrate that death rates from coronary heart disease are lower among consumers of small amounts of alcohol than among non-drinkers the net effect of the reported consumption of small to moderate amounts of alcohol is a reduction in total mortality of the drinking population'.*

The results of research by Sir Richard Doll and Professor Leon Simons find conclusively that there is a net health and cost benefit to our society from consuming wine in moderation. This calls for a reassessment by those in the health industry who hold the view that alcohol and good health are not good companions.

A key to overall better health in our society in the future lies in educating the young about good health. This should include advice on wise drinking habits, such as the sensible, moderate consumption of wine to help prevent vascular disease. We must through education minimise the harm to individuals through the abuse of alcohol, while not penalising or discouraging the vast majority of people who gain enjoyment and health benefits from the consumption of wine in moderation. We must distinguish between drinking wine in moderation and abusing wine through binge drinking, or consuming an excessive amount in a short time.

*"Wherever wine is lacking, drugs become necessary."*
*Jewish Talmud.*

# GLOSSARY

ALZHEIMER'S DISEASE The most common form of dementia, named after the doctor who described the disease, where brain tissue is gradually replaced by scar tissue.

ANEURYSM Large dilation of an artery which may later leak or burst open.

ANTI SCORBUTICS Substances which counter scurvy or lack of vitamin C.

AORTA Largest artery in the body which takes blood from the heart to the abdomen.

CEREBRAL VASCULAR ACCIDENT (CVA) Medical term for a stroke or death of brain tissue due to lack of blood supply to that tissue.

CIRRHOSIS OF THE LIVER Scar tissue formation in the liver, usually due to excessive alcohol consumption.

DEEP VEIN THROMBOSIS (DVT) Clot in a deep major vein in the leg.

DEMENTIA A global loss of higher brain (thought and reasoning) function.

KORSAKOFF'S SYNDROME Degeneration of the brain causing permanent short term memory loss, confusion and disorientation due to vitamin B deficiency. Especially seen in alcohol abuse.

INFARCTION Blockage of a blood vessel resulting in tissue death.

ISCHAEMIA A lack of blood flowing through a blood vessel, but not bad enough to cause tissue death.

MACULAR DEGENERATION A cause of blindness, where nerves in the light sensing area at the back of the eye (the retina), degenerate and die off.

M.A.P. KINASE Mitogen Activated Protein Kinase enzyme, is a proactive enzyme cascade, forming one of the main intracellular (within the cell) signalling pathways.

MYOCARDITIS Inflammation of the heart muscle of which the most common cause is a viral infection. Excessive alcohol consumption is also a cause.

MYOCARDOPATHY Permanent damage to heart muscle such that it won't contract properly, leading to heart failure.

NEUROPATHY Loss of sensation and sometimes function, due to a damaged nerve. Excessive alcohol consumption is a common cause.

PANCREATITIS Inflammation of the pancreas. Excessive alcohol consumption is a common cause.

PARKINSON'S DISEASE A disease of the basal ganglion part of the brain, due to a lack of the neuro-transmitter dopamine (the chemical that makes the nerves fire off), resulting in stiffness and shakes.

PERIPHERAL NEUROPATHY Damage to the nerves of the limbs, one cause of which is excessive alcohol consumption.

ULCER A break in the lining of a tissue (usually the stomach wall or skin), resulting in a shallow wide hole.

WERNICKE'S ENCEPHALOPATHY Degeneration of the brain, causing multiple nerve palsies (nerves that don't work), involving eyes and balance mechanism. Especially seen in alcohol abuse, due to vitamin B deficiency.

# REFERENCES

Becker et al. 1996, 'Prediction of risk of liver disease by alcohol intake, sex and age', *Hepatology*, vol. 23, pp.1025–1029.

Bellantani et al. 1997, 'Drinking habits as cofactors of risk for alcohol induced liver damage', *Gut,* vol. 41, pp. 845–850.

Cullen et al. 1982, 'Alcohol and mortality in the Busselton study', *International Journal of Epidemiology*, vol. 11, pp.67–70.

Cullen et al: 'Alcohol and Mortality in Busselton, Western Australia', *American Journal Epidemiology*, vol. 137, No. 2, pp. 242–248.

Doll et al. 1994, 'Mortality in relation to consumption of alcohol: 13 years observations on male British doctors', *British Medical Journal*, vol. 39, pp. 911–918.

Doll, R. 1997, 'One for the heart', *British Medical Journal*, no. 315, pp. 1664–1668.

Ellison, R.C. 1995, 'Does moderate alcohol consumption prolong life?', *American Council on Science and Health, Inc.*

Frankel, E.N. 1994, 'Red wine antioxidants and potential health benefits', paper presented to the Society of Medical Friends of Wine, Mark Hopkins Intercontinental Hotel, San Francisco.

Gronbaek, M. et al. 1994,'Influence of sex, age, body mass index, and smoking on alcohol intake and mortality', *British Medical Journal*, vol. 308, pp. 302–308.

Gronbaek, M. et al. 1995, 'Mortality associated with moderate intake of wine, beer or spirits', *British Medical Journal*, vol. 310, pp. 1165–1168.

Jackson, et al. 1985, 'Alcohol consumption and blood pressure', *American Journal of Epidemiology*, vol. 122, no. 6, pp. 1037–1044.

Jackson, et al. 1991, 'Alcohol consumption and risk of coronary heart disease', *British Medical Journal*, vol. 33, pp 211–216.

Jung, K. et al. 1999, 'Moderate red and white wine consumption and the risk of cardiovascular disease', Herz/Kreislauf, no. 31, pp. 25–31.

Kaplan, N.M. 1991, 'Bashing booze: the danger of losing the benefits of moderate alcohol consumption', *American Heart Journal,* vol. 121, No 6, pp. 1854–1856.

Marmot, M. et al. 1991, 'Alcohol and cardiovascular disease: the status of the U shaped curve', *British Medical Journal,* vol. 303, pp. 565–568.

ME Magazine, 1997, 'A drink a day can keep a heart attack away', *Jordan Heart Research Foundation,* p. 21.

Orgogozo, J.M. 1997, 'Wine consumption and dementia in the elderly: A prospective community study in the Bordeaux area', *Rev. Neurol* (Paris), vol. 153 (3), pp. 185–192.

Polygenis, D. Wharton, S. Malmberg, C. et al. 1998, 'Moderate alcohol consumption during pregnancy and the incidence of foetal malformations: A meta-analysis', *Neurotoxicology Teratol* no. 20, pp. 61–67.

Renaud, S. & DeLorgeril, M. 1992, 'Wine, alcohol, platelets, and the French paradox for coronary heart disease', *The Lancet,* vol 339, pp. 1523–1526.

Renaud, S. et al. 1998, 'Alcohol and mortality in middle-aged men from eastern France', *Epidemiology,* vol. 9, no. 2, pp

Rimm, et al. 1991, 'Prospective study of alcohol consumption and risk of coronary disease in men', *The Lancet,* vol. 338, pp. 464–468.

Rodgers, et al. 1993, 'Alcohol and stroke, a case - control study of drinking habits past and present', *Stroke,* vol. 24, pp. 1473–1477.

Simons, et al. 1996, 'Predictors of mortality in the prospective Dubbo study of Australian elderly', *Australia & New-Zealand Journal Medicine,* vol. 26, pp. 40–48.

Simons, et al. 1996, 'Alcohol intake and survival in the elderly: a 77 month follow-up in the Dubbo study', *Australia & New-Zealand Journal Medicine,* vol. 26, pp. 662–670.

Skurray, G. 1998, *Wine Making Practice and Resveratrol in Wine ,* Centre for Advanced Food Research, University of Western Sydney, Hawkesbury.

Stampfer, et al. 1988, 'A prospective study of moderate alcohol consumption and the risk of coronary disease and stroke in women', *New England Journal of Medicine,* vol. 319, pp. 267–273.

Stockley, C.S. 1998, Wine in Moderation: How Could and Should Recent in Vitro and in Vivo Data be Interpreted?, paper presented at the 2nd International Conference on drinking patterns and their consequences, Curtin University.

Troup, G.J. 1995, 'Free radical scavenging abilities of beverages', *International Journal of Food Science and Technology,* vol. 30, pp. 535–537.

UK Department of Health, *Sensible Drinking.*

US Department of Health and Human Services 1995, *Nutrition and Your Health: Dietary Guidelines for Americans.*

Vinson, J.A. & Hontz, B.A. 1995, 'Phenol antioxidant index: comparative antioxidant effectiveness of red and white wines', *Journal of Agricultural & Food Chemistry,* vol. 43, pp. 401–403.

Walpole, et al. 1990, 'Is there a foetal effect with low to moderate alcohol use before or during pregnancy?', *Journal of Epidemiology and Community Health,* vol. 44, pp. 297–301.